FRANCISCAN WARE

by
Delleen Enge

Photography by James R. Berube

COLLECTOR BOOKS
P.O. Box 3009
Paducah, KY 42001

The current values in this book should be used only as a guide. They are not intended to set prices, which vary from one section of the country to another. Auction prices as well as dealer prices vary greatly and are affected by condition as well as demand. Neither the Author nor the Publisher assumes responsibility for any losses that might be incurred as a result of consulting this guide.

Additional copies of this book may be ordered from:

COLLECTOR BOOKS
P.O. Box 3009
Paducah, Kentucky 42001
or
The Author, Delleen Enge
912 N. Signal Street
Ojai, CA 93023

@ $9.95 Add $1.00 for postage and handling.

Printed by IMAGE GRAPHICS, Paducah, Kentucky

About The Author

Delleen Enge is a native Californian and the mother of three daughters. She has a B.S. degree from Southern Oregon College, a M.S. from University of Oregon and did graduate work at UCLA and California State University, Northridge. She has been a teacher of Special Children at Nordhoff High School in Ojai, California, for sixteen years.

She was raised with Franciscan ware in her parents home and it continued in her own home and also the homes of her three daughters. Her continuing admiration for the beauty and quality of Franciscan ware led her into becoming a collector for many years and hence the desire to pass her knowledge on to others by writing this book.

Dedication

This book is dedicated to all the faithful employees who have worked so many years to produce such exceptional ware.

Gladding, McBean & Company were famous for their hand decorated tile.

Acknowledgements

C.C. Lovewell, my neighbor, took pictures and got me started. Jim Berube, Dean of Students at the local high school, and a very patient man, did all the photography unless otherwise noted.

Marion Murphy, my friend, kept me company while driving all over looking for Franciscan (she hates stores unless they have books).

My good friend, Dorothy Higgins, insisted I get busy. She typed the letters to Franciscan when it was owned by Interpace to ask permission and to gain entrance into the plant. She has also done all the typing and retyping to get the book ready.

My three daughters, Carlleen, Kathy, and Merrianne, have been most supportive in helping with the research.

The first time I called the Franciscan plant for an appointment, I was referred to Jean Naper, Mr. George V. Najor's secretary. Since she's put up with me for the last 3½ years we have become good friends. Mr. Najor, head of the dinnerware department had worked at the plant for 41 years. He retired in September, 1978. He is such a quiet, polite person and never got upset with all my questions and all the dishes I brought for identification. Upon occasion, it is necessary for me to phone Mr. Najor at his home when I need encouragement and facts that only he knows. If we really had a difficult piece, he would call Katie Giannoni or Jim Ryan and they always came up with the answer.

Upon Mr. Najor's retirement, Arthur L. Stein became head of the department and began placating me. He is still helping with all my many problems, and a great many of the pictures are due to his help.

Whenever I visit the plant, which is a two hour drive from my home, it is always a great experience. They treat me so nicely, just as if I really were someone special. I don't believe it. In fact, I tell people "Whenever I get feeling sorry for myself, I just go to Franciscan and they make me feel ten feet tall!"

In 1979, when Wedgwood bought the plant I figured that it would be the end of me. What a surprise when Mr. Ken Johnston was really interested in the book writing project. Then when Mr. Ian Taylor wrote that he wanted to see me, I was apprehensive that my project was about to come to an end. To my astonishment, he called me in to encourage the completion and to offer help.

People who helped me gather Franciscan ware are Connie Blum, Garbo's Pottery, Sally Groves, Cliff Hay, Jean Hayes, Meg Houley, Sharon Jarell, Florence & Leo Keopples, Maria McManus, E. Majeskey, Lillian Miller, Carol Mueller, Maureen Popp, Vonna Sharon, Veronica Sanford, Marion Suway, Bob Thayer, Kathy Tocchini.

Contents

Foreword

What prompted me to compile this information? I think it was the fact that Fiesta, Bauer, Vernon and some of the others were getting the limelight and the love of my life, the best pottery of all, Franciscan, was being ignored!

Why was Franciscan my favorite? I grew up with it. We used it in our home. My mother bought seconds at the factory for our school cafeteria. Our high school had no kiln so our teacher took the unfired clay projects to Gladding, McBean and they fired them for us. (Imagine anything like this happening today.) Of course, this was back in the 1930's. We visited the factory often and are still a Franciscan family today.

My sister and I both had Franciscan given to us as wedding gifts and thirty-five years later we are still using them. We both have the Coronado pattern. She has coral and turquoise in the satin finish and I have the ivory. My daughter, Kathy, has almost all the pieces of Coronado in turquoise satin which she uses daily. She laments she is probably the only person alive that has had to wash the same kind of dishes her whole life, but she loves them. My mother Kathleen Ruddell, just sent some pieces down from Oregon so I could have them photographed. She has been using them since 1934.

This book is an attempt to bring Franciscan to the attention of collectors as there are so many unknown patterns of dinnerware. They were far ahead of their time during the period of 1934 to 1950, but due to the economy, poor advertising and a lack of public awareness, the beautiful hand painted and hand crafted dinnerware was not widely known.

Franciscan History

Franciscan was so named in honor of the Franciscan Padres who came to California in the 1700's. They were great builders of sturdy structures, as the missions they built along our California coast are still in use today. I am sure some Franciscan ware will be in use that long also.

Franciscan really had its beginning back in 1875 when three entrepreneurs from Chicago, Charles Gladding, Peter McBean and George Chambers found out about the clay in Placer County, California.

Placer County, in northern California, extends from the Sacramento Valley to the Nevada State line in the Sierra Nevadas. Its' name was taken from the richness of the gold placers. It was a mining county until 1890 when fruit farming for shipment to the east was developed. With Gladding, McBean & Company producing clay products, by 1920 the value of their products far exceeded both gold and agriculture. Even today, the town of Lincoln, in Placer County, evolves around the Gladding, McBean Pottery Works. This would make another book in itself, and it would be very exciting. Many of the public buildings in Lincoln were built by Gladding, McBean & Company; the swimming pool, the library and the woman's club to mention a few.

Gladding, McBean & Company started with a capital investment of $12,000, really less as the eastern paper money had to be converted into western gold at a large discount. They formed a company and first manufactured clay sewer pipe and face brick with the loam clay.

Gladding, McBean & Company had a great impact in the development of the use of clay in architecture as well as other innovative products. The company was known for its wide use of Terra Cotta.

Terra Cotta was used in the construction of the twenty-six story telephone building and the thirty story Russ Building in San Francisco. Los Angeles was noted for its outstanding use of Terra Cotta.

Hollow tile was first produced at Lincoln in 1890 and face brick in 1891. These fireproof materials were much in demand to the builders in San Francisco.

The Crocker Building and Mills Building in San Francisco and the courthouse of King, Washington and Los Angeles County prominently displayed floors made of the hollow tile.

Enameled brick was first made for the walls of the court of the Flood Building and the Post Office in San Francisco in 1899. Coated brick was developed in 1915. Granitex was first used for the San Francisco Public Library.

Two of California's greatest contributions to the artistic world of architecture was Gladding, McBean & Company's cordova roof tile and decorative wall and fireplace tile. Stanford University is an example of the roof tile.

Around 1922, Gladding, McBean & Company wanted to expand. They made a few Terra Cotta plates as experiments. I have one of these plates that was given to me by John Perry who started work at the Lincoln plant when he was eight years old and worked there for fifty-two years. I visited with him and his wife in 1978. They are such a lovely couple and so friendly and giving. I learned so many interesting things from them.

In doing this research one of the things that amazed me the most was the great length of time various people had worked for Gladding, McBean & Company at both the Lincoln and the Los Angeles plants. Some of the hand painters, production people and others have been there thirty-seven years or more. Many people have only worked for this one enterprise.

In 1922, Gladding, McBean & Company purchased Tropico Pottery which had been manufacturing decorative pottery and floor tile

8

in Glendale, California since 1904. This is the site that houses the present day Franciscan plant. After the acquisition, a distinguished group of artists and highly trained technicians were assembled to expand the already successful business. Their tile manufacture was acclaimed throughout the United States and other parts of the world. In 1933, the West Coast properties of American Eucastic Tile Company with two well-equipped plants became part of the Gladding, McBean & Company. Whenever a western architect or designer required a ceramic material of durability and quality, they generally presented their problem to Gladding, McBean & Company. They had the largest and most knowledgeable staff of any ceramic producer in the world.

In November, 1933, Atholl McBean met with Fredrick Grant II, a chemical engineer from Zaneville, Ohio, who at one time had been president of the Weller Pottery Company. In January of 1934, he was hired as manager of the new dinnerware department of Gladding, McBean & Company.

Mrs. Mary M. Grant, a former art director of Macy's in New York, helped her husband by designing many magnificient patterns, some still being produced at present. She worked from 1934 but was not put on the payroll until 1938.

The manufacture of dinnerware began in 1934, and was dedicated to the development of a superior product. The first earthen dinnerware was in six bright colors; soon other bright colors were added, as well as pastels. As time went on many unusual designs and shapes were produced. Today these would be an even greater success than they were then. They were too far ahead of the time, and lack of advertising caused some patterns to have a short production period. From 1933 to 1939 there were fourteen different patterns besides all the Art Ware. I am sure Mary Grant was inspirational through this era. There is much more to be said concerning the people who designed, labored, managed and believed.

Franciscan Earthenware is made from a material called "Malinite", which was developed by the chemists of Gladding, McBean & Company, and which is covered by a number of U.S. and foreign patents. "Malinite" is the most important technical achievement in the pottery industry in the past century. Instead of wares being made from clay, the basic material of the "Malinite" body is talc rock, the same material from which talcum powder is produced. Combined with the talc is an emorphous flux which in the heat of the kiln so binds together the molecules of talc that an extremely tough and durable body is formed, highly resistant to thermal shock and free from internal flows. The most important feature of "Malinite" is the fact that glazes become so fused with the body that they cannot craze. Another glaze feature lies in the brilliant palette of colors and inimitable matte textures that can be produced.

9

Gladding, McBean & Company
Products and Patterns

	Year Discontinued
1934 Tropico Art Ware	1937
Garden Ware	1936
Cielito Art Ware	1937
Cocinero Ware	1938
Florist and Florist Special	1941
Coronado Art Ware	1942
Coronado Table Ware	1954
El Patio Table and Art Ware	1953
1935 El Patio Nuevo	1936
Franciscan Ruby Art Ware	1936
1936 Capistrano Art Ware	1942
1937 Avalon Art Ware	1942
Aurora Art Ware	1942
Catalina Art Ware	1941
Encanto Art Ware	1939
Montecito Table Ware	1942
Padua I (Underglaze deco, MP7)	1942
Rancho Table Ware (Catalina)	1940
Del Mar	1938
Del Oro	1938
Mango	1938
Willow	1942
1938 Kitchen Ware (succeeds Cocinero)	1941
Ox Blood Art Ware	1942
Hawthorne	1942
Fruit (light blue and blue decal)	1939
Encanto Art Ware	1940
1939 Geranium	1942

The Dinnerwares

The dinnerwares will be presented in the order of the year produced. I have tried to use at least one of each color that I have, but I am still lacking many colors and many shapes in all areas. When I use the term orange, it means orange like the fruit and when I say red, it means red like an apple.

This brightly colored pottery had its beginning in California. I will start with the first produced by Gladding, McBean & Company in 1934. This was their El Patio line. The name suggests a patio party. The bright colors would enhance any festive occasion or perhaps make a dull affair have a warmer feeling. There are over 103 shapes and twenty different colors in this ever popular pattern. The handles on the cups and bowls are very distinctive. Someone once described them as "prezel-shaped." Just when I become discouraged and think I will never find a piece I do not have, lo and behold another will surface from an unknown source!

Another pattern started in 1934 and perhaps the best known of the older dinnerware is Coronado. Many of you refer to it as the "Swirl." It had well over sixty shapes and fifteen colors. There was also an Art Ware line in Coronado. Some of the pieces might be listed on both sections. They can be intermingled nicely. The Coronado dinnerware shown in this book is perhaps the most complete collection.

In 1935 a new line of El Patio was started and called El Patio Nuevo. It was a two-tone pattern. One color combination was turquoise on the inside and white on the outside. The other color was Chinese yellow on the inside and white on the outside. Some of the shapes are used in other sets which will be pointed out in the pictures. These were made for only one year which could be one reason I have yet to find any,

In 1937, the Ranch Table Ware, which was one of the lines purchased from Catalina, was produced in Glendale (Los Angeles now). It came in eleven colors and twenty-eight or more shapes. These molds were adapted to other sets of dinnerware.

The Montecito Table Ware was also started in 1937. This was made in seventeen colors or color combinations. The pastels were very subtle, especially those in the satin glaze. The gloss glazes are beautiful. The shapes are pleasing and give a formal feeling. There were over fifty shapes in this pattern, some very elegant. The handle shapes, the rim on the edge of the plates and bowls, and the two ridges at the bottom of the cups, bowls and pots and on the inside of the plates are all clues for identifying this pattern.

Padua was another 1937 creation and is one of my personal favorites. It was produced in six color combinations with approx-

11

imately thirty-two shapes. There was a buff color and a celadon color produced exclusively for Barker Brothers in California. The Padua was the first hand decorated earthenware produced by Franciscan. All of the Padua has a delicate china feeling.

The Mango, a hand decorated under glaze, is a bright orange with brown trim. Here again, a beautiful quality in around twenty shapes.

The Del Oro is striking with a beautiful Chinese yellow center with a transparent glaze around the edge. It was produced in thirty various shapes.

The beautiful sky blue Del Mar, with its whimsical hand painted little white sail boats and darker blue glaze designed to represent waves, would be a sell out if available now. It was produced only from 1937-1938 and in about 116 shapes. It was simply ahead of its time.

Another 1937 creation and truly unusual was the Willow. It had a hand decorated stylized little tree centered in the dinnerware. It was produced in two colors with less than twenty shapes.

One of the most unique of the 1937 productions was the Tiger Flower. This one has to be seen to be really appreciated. It has gorgeous white flowers and almost feels like enamel, with either a coral or celadon background in eighteen or more shapes.

A line with a greater variety of pieces was the Hawthorne. It was oriental-looking and hand decorated with a spray of flowers in the center. This line came on the market about 1938.

Another 1938 line is the ever popular Fruit motif. This pattern came in a dark and light blue, or a brown on a yellow background. This was also a centered design produced in around twenty shapes.

My chosen prize winner for 1939 was the Geranium. This was part decal and part hand decorated. The color combinations were unbelievable; reds and maroons. This was another pattern that was too advanced for its time, but I am sure would be a great success to-day.

12

El Patio
1934-1954

El Patio was one of Franciscan's larger lines and was produced in 105 different shapes and twenty colors, in both the gloss and satin glazes.

All pictures will be identified from left to right and bottom to top.

Front Row:

    Onion soup with tab handles in golden glow gloss $ 3.00- 7.00

    Oval serving bowl, turquoise gloss . . . . $ 6.00- 8.00

    Individual fruit, turquoise satin . . . . $ 3.00- 5.00

Second Row:

    Cereal or soup, apple green gloss . . . . $ 5.00- 7.00

    Cereal or soup, turquoise gloss . . . . $ 5.00- 7.00

    Cereal or soup, orange gloss . . . . $ 5.00- 7.00

Top Row:

    Chop plate, redwood gloss glaze . . . . $ 8.00-20.00

Front Row:

    Coral satin dessert plate . . . . $ 3.50- 6.00

    Gray satin 8¼″ salad plate . . . . $ 3.50- 6.00

    Yellow gloss glaze 9½″ luncheon plate . . . . $ 4.00- 7.00

Top Row:

    Apple green 14″ chop plate . . . . $ 8.00-20.00

14

Front Row:
    10½" lettuce green dinner plate . . . . $ 7.00-10.00
    Ivory satin 6¼" bread and butter plate . . . . $ 3.50- 6.00
Top Row:
    12" chop plate in turquoise gloss . . . . $ 7.00-18.00

15

Front Row:
  Round serving bowl, 8½″ diameter, turquoise
    gloss .... $ 4.00- 9.00
  Baking dish with lid (they do not match) .... $ 3.50- 8.50
  Round serving, 9″ diameter, chartreuse gloss ... $ 4.00-13.00
Top Row:
  Large serving bowl, 10½″ light yellow satin ..... $ 8.00-20.00
  Salad bowl, 4″ high, 9½″ diameter, turquoise gloss $ 9.00-24.00

Front Row:

> Sherbet or double egg cup, maroon gloss . . . . $ 2.00- 6.00
> Cream pitcher, turquoise gloss . . . . $ 4.00- 6.00
> Jam jar with lid, light yellow . . . . $ 6.00-10.00
> Sugar with lid, turquoise gloss . . . . $ 5.00- 8.00
> Cream soup cup and saucer, turquoise gloss . . . . $ 9.00-18.00

Top Row:

> This cup and matching saucer are the only pieces
>   I have ever found in eggplant color (notice the
>   cup handle) . . . . $ 7.00-14.00
> Pitcher in two colors, white satin on the outside
>   and maroon on the inside $10.00-20.00
> Relish dish with handle, three compartments . . . $ 7.00-12.00

Front Row:
> Six cup teapot (should have lid), Mexican blue
> gloss .... $ 9.00-18.00
> Six cup teapot, a later shape (should have a dome-
> shaped lid), coral satin .... $ 9.00-18.00
> Syrup pitcher (it did not have a lid), turquoise
> gloss .... $ 4.00- 9.00
> Water jug, ball shape, coral satin .... $ 7.00-18.00

Top Row:
> Toby Mug jug, 7½″ tall, 3½″ across bottom,
> maroon gloss $10.00-20.00
> 2½ quart pitcher with ice lip, turquoise gloss ... $ 9.00-15.00

This picture shows the development of the gravy boat.
The first one produced was the top center, which had
     an unattached underplate .... $ 9.00-12.00
On the left is the plate with an attached underplate,
     which was difficult to produce .... $ 8.00-16.00
The gray gravy boat on the right has the base lowered
     and plate attached .... $ 9.00-16.00

Front Row:
    Party plate with cup well, golden glow . . . . $ 4.00- 6.00
    Salt and pepper, orange gloss . . . . $ 5.00- 9.00
    Party plate with cup, redwood . . . . $ 8.00-14.00
Top Row:
    An oval platter, 13″, golden glow gloss . . . . $ 9.00-18.00
    Candleholder, satin ivory . . . . $ 8.00-10.00

The first and the last in this row are called Gurnsey jugs and are
5½" tall. The lid goes into the jug ¾" and has a V-cut in one place.
The lid can be turned to close the jug. A very unique idea to seal.

Gurnsey jug . . . . $ 8.00-18.00
Syrup or hot water with a lid . . . . $ 8.00-14.00
Tea tile, Mexican blue gloss, fits under the various
    pots . . . . $ 8.00-10.00
Syrup pitcher, Mexican blue gloss . . . . $ 8.00-10.00
Gurnsey jug . . . . $ 8.00-18.00

Front Row:
Notice the various handles on these tumblers. Apple green gloss, light yellow gloss, turquoise gloss, redwood gloss, Mexican blue gloss, ivory satin, and dark yellow gloss.

Tumblers with handles .... $ 6.00-10.00
Without handles .... $ 4.00- 8.00

Top Row:
Tumbler, golden glow gloss .... $ 4.00-10.00
Redwood Coffee server with iron frame $12.00-20.00
Orange tumbler .... $ 4.00-10.00

These shapes are from the later years.

    Creamer . . . . $ 4.00- 8.00
    Coffee pot (the lid was dome-shaped) . . . . $ 8.00-12.00
    Sugar. . . . . $ 4.00- 8.00

Large covered casserole, 9½″ diameter, 4″ high,
  apple green gloss $22.00-32.00

Coronado Table Ware
1936-1956

The Coronado table ware was produced in fifteen colors in both gloss and satin glazes and in over fifty different shapes.

All pictures will be identified from left to right, and from bottom to top.

Front Row:

9½" plate, gray satin	$	4.00- 7.00
8½" plate, light yellow gloss	$	5.00- 7.00
7½" plate, ivory satin	$	5.00- 7.00
6½" plate, maroon gloss	$	3.00- 4.00

Top Row:

10½" dinner plate, coral gloss	$	8.00-16.00

14" Round serving plate, redwood gloss .... $ 9.00-14.00
Plate for bones or salad, ivory gloss .... $ 7.00-12.00
12½" chop plate, ivory satin .... $ 8.00-14.00

15½" Oval platter, turquoise gloss $14.00-20.00
13" Oval platter, light yellow satin $10.00-13.00
10" Oval platter, celadon satin . . . . $ 9.00-12.00

Front Row:
    Cereal bowl, light yellow gloss . . . . $ 4.00- 7.00

    Onion soup with tab handles and a lid, coral gloss . $ 6.00-10.00

    Sherbet or egg cup, turquoise satin . . . . $ 5.00- 8.00

    Individual fruit or vegetable, coral satin . . . . $ 3.00- 5.00

Top Row:
    Flat soup, light yellow gloss . . . . $ 6.00- 8.00

    Small nutcup, turquoise gloss . . . . $ 9.00-14.00

    Flat soup, ivory satin . . . . $ 6.00- 8.00

Front Row:
    Round serving dish, coral satin . . . . $ 6.00- 9.00
    Oval serving dish, turquoise gloss . . . . $ 7.00-10.00
    Casserole and lid, coral satin . . . . $ 9.00-13.00
Top Row:
    Round serving dish, ivory satin . . . . $ 8.00-12.00
    Round serving dish, maroon gloss . . . . $ 9.00-13.00

Large salad bowl and plate, apple green gloss . . . $20.00-25.00

Tea set in beautiful white gloss, original design with high
pedestal base. Later the base was removed as it was easier and less
costly to produce.

Creamer $10.00-15.00
Teapot................................... $20.00-30.00
Sugar.................................... $10.00-15.00

After dinner coffee pot and cups or chocolate set.

Coffee or chocolate pot $18.00-20.00
Cup . . . . $ 5.00- 8.00
Saucer . . . . $ 2.00- 3.00

Teapot without pedestal base, turquoise gloss . . . $10.00-15.00
Pitcher, turquoise gloss $14.00-16.00

Front Row:

Oval relish dish with a handle at one end, maroon
gloss .... $ 8.00-10.00
Cream pitcher, turquoise gloss .... $ 6.00- 8.00
Butter and cover, coral satin $10.00-14.00

Top Row:

Sugar with lid, coral gloss .... $ 7.00-10.00
Salt and pepper, turquoise gloss .... $ 5.00- 7.00
Gravy with an attached plate, yellow satin $15.00-20.00

Front Row:
> Cream soup cup and saucer (the saucer is larger
> than the regular saucer) yellow gloss
>> Cup .... $ 8.00-10.00
>> Saucer .... $ 3.00- 4.00
> Demi-tasse cup and saucer, maroon gloss
>> Cup $10.00-12.00
>> Saucer .... $ 3.00- 5.00
> Cup to fit into the well on the crescent-shaped
>> hostess plate, turquoise gloss .... $ 2.00- 4.00
>> Hostess plate $10.00-12.00

Top Row:
> Cup and saucer, coral satin
>> Cup .... $ 3.00- 4.00
>> Saucer .... $ 1.00- 2.00
> Jumbo cup, maroon gloss .... $ 8.50-10.50
> Saucer, turquoise gloss .... $ 3.00- 5.00

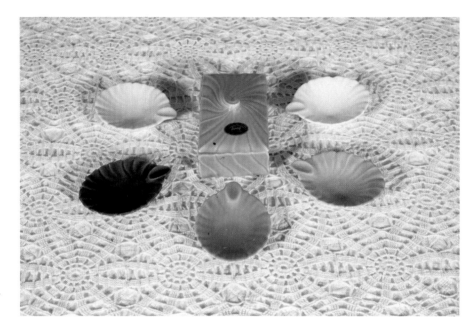

Cigarette box with original paper label, turquoise
  gloss $20.00-30.00
Shell shaped ash trays .... each $3.00- 4.00

Montecito Table Ware
1937-1942

The Montecito table ware was produced in seventeen colors, or color combinations, with more than forty-five shapes. All pictures will be identified from left to right, and from bottom to top.

Front Row:

Egg cup, coral satin	$ 3.00- 5.00
Cream pitcher, light yellow	$ 4.00- 6.00
Sherbet, light blue	$ 6.00- 8.00
Sugar bowl, red	$ 4.00- 6.00
Sugar, celadon satin, which is most unusual	$ 4.00- 6.00

Top Row:

Large cream pitcher	$ 5.00- 7.00
Sugar bowl with lid	$ 7.00- 9.00
Gravy with the plate attached, coral gloss	$ 7.00- 9.00

Front Row:

    10½'' Dinner plate, turquoise gloss . . . . $ 7.00-10.00

    8½'' Dessert plate . . . . $ 5.00- 6.00

    Cream soup cup with saucer, light blue . . . . $ 6.00- 8.00

    7½'' Salad plate, light green . . . . $ 4.00- 5.00

    9½'' Luncheon plate, light gray . . . . $ 6.00- 8.00

Top Row:

    Cup with two colors, celadon and copper gloss . . $10.00-12.00

    Tumbler, turquoise gloss . . . . $ 6.00- 8.00

    Salt and pepper . . . . $ 6.00- 8.00

Front Row:

    Hot water pot, light blue gloss $10.00-12.00

    Teapot, light blue gloss $10.00-12.00

    Individual teapot, turquoise gloss . . . . $ 8.00-10.00

    Individual hot water pot, turquoise gloss . . . . $ 8.00-10.00

Top Row:

    Hexagonal bowl with handles, 6¼" high and 11"

      across $40.00-50.00

Padua Table Ware
1937-1940

A beautiful color combination of the natural clay color with a transparent glaze. Padua table ware was hand decorated usually with browns and yellows. There were also other colors made with the same design in a light blue and celadon.

On this breakfast table we will start in the back.

Toast cover	$20.00-25.00
Cream jug	$12.00-14.00
Sugar with lid (notice the handles)	$ 9.00-12.00
Tab handled cereal	$ 6.00- 8.00
9½" plate	$ 7.00-10.00
Egg cup (setting on 6½" plate)	$ 6.00- 8.00
6½" plate	$ 4.00- 6.00
Cup	$ 6.00- 8.00
Saucer	$ 2.00- 4.00
Salt and pepper	$ 9.00-12.00
Tumbler	$ 7.00-12.00
Coffee jug and stopper	$14.00-18.00
Standing in the back is a 12" plate	$14.00-18.00

Around the edge of the table, left to right:

Tea pot (early shape) $14.00-18.00
Covered onion soup with original label $10.00-12.00
Individual tea pot (lid missing) $10.00-12.00
Tea pot (new shape) $12.00-14.00
A & D coffee pot $16.00-18.00

Center:

Covered casserole $20.00-25.00

Back:

14" Console bowl $20.00-23.00
Serving bowl $14.00-18.00

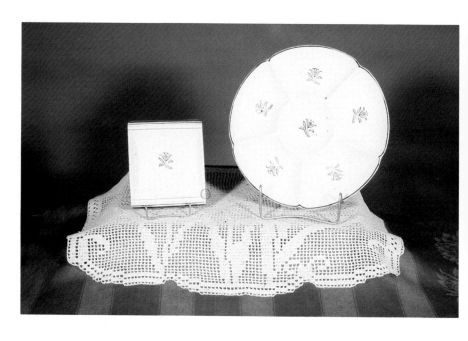

Square dish, unusual $20.00-25.00
Hors d'ouvre tray, unusual $35.00-40.00

Large bowl in celadon glaze $35.00-40.00

There are no valid prices at the present time on Del Mar, Del Oro, Mango, Willow, Rancho, Tiger Flower, Hawthorne, Fruit, or Geranium table ware.

Del Mar Table Ware
1937-1938

Del Mar table ware was made from the same molds as the El Patio line. They were made in light blue and the decoration was done by hand.

Del Oro
1937-1939

These were made from the same molds as the Montecito line. The color was deemed Chinese yellow and white. They are of beautiful quality. There were twenty-eight different shapes made in this set.

Mango Table Ware
1937-1938

These are of the same shapes as the Del Oro and Montecito. They are hand painted and then a clear glaze over the entire piece. They are of exceptional quality and design.

Rancho Table Ware
1937-1941

The Rancho table ware was all produced from molds that Gladding, McBean & Co. purchased from the Catalina Island Pottery Co. They are usually stamped Catalina-Rancho on the bottom (see section on marks). This was a large line with over fifty-three shapes. There were eight sizes of round plates.

Willow Table Ware
1937 to July, 1940

Such a beautiful stylized tree made in only the two colors. The brown under light yellow and the blue in oatmeal satin.

Tiger Flower Table Ware
1937-1942

Heavy enamel-like hand painted flowers; it came in only two colors, coral and celadon.

Fruit Table Ware
1938-1942

This came blue on blue and brown on light yellow. Very nice. There were over eighteen shapes in this set.

Hawthorne Table Ware
1938-1942

Very oriental looking and very well executed. Notice we still have the same shapes with a different motif. A new decorating method was used. The design was hand stamped and then hand decorated. This is a transparent glaze over all.

Geranium Table Ware
1939-1942

This was another new method of decorating. It involved three parts–a hand stamp, hand decoration and some decal. The colors are startling in bright red and maroon.

Art Ware

The first pottery plant bought by Gladding, McBean & Co. when they decided to extend their operations in 1923, was the Tropico Pottery on Los Feliz Boulevard where the big plant is at present. Tropico made garden supplies and florist supplies, huge urns, bird baths, fountains and a line of kitchen ware like mixing bowls, range sets, etc.

Many vase shapes were carried from one series name to another and were glazed or decorated to fit that particular need. I have not always rephotographed when the same shape is carried to another line unless the color is different. Sometimes the same shape is in five different groups. For example, a large low pedestal bowl was a Catalina mold; therefore, it was in the line called Catalina, and was glazed in many single colors. The same shape was in the Avalon Art Ware line, and was glazed in either ivory satin or turquoise satin inside and ivory satin outside. It could also be found in the Aurora Art Ware with turquoise gloss inside and ivory satin outside. So you can understand how confusing this can be.

Cielito Art Ware was made from 1934-1937. It was made with two colors on each piece; either ivory satin and turquoise gloss or Chinese yellow and white. I have none of this to show. This pattern is the same as the Coronado dinner ware but was not made in as many colors. I have found pieces made in colors other than what the research indicated. The colors listed in the research were ivory satin, coral satin, turquoise satin and dark yellow. The candle holders I found are celadon, and the round box with a lid is light yellow. We must look at the shapes for identification. There were at least twenty-eight shapes; all very useful and well designed.

Franciscan Ruby Art Ware was made only one year from 1935 to 1936. There were around twenty different shapes, eleven were vases and nine were other things such as tea and coffee pots, sugar, creamer, candle holders, cup and saucer, salt and pepper, and a bowl. These are strikingly beautiful; the red is so brilliant. They are very delicate, not heavy. Seeing is believing.

Capistrano Art Ware was another pottery works Gladding, McBean & Company bought. This line was produced from 1936 through 1942. There were forty-five or so molds with almost the same number of colors and color combinations. The glazes were all developed by the chemists at Gladding, McBean & Company. The most unusual color combination being an egg plant color inside, and blue satin outside. There were some very different shapes, one being the Goose in oatmeal. He is really quite charming.

Avalon Art Ware was produced from 1938 to 1942 and were all made from Catalina molds using Gladding, McBean glazes. There are about twenty in this line. Some of you will very readily observe the well known Catalina shapes.

Aurora Art Ware pieces are all from Catalina molds and this group has about twenty-three in it. Many shapes are repeated from Avalon, but with a different glaze.

Catalina Art Ware produced from 1937 until 1941 was by far the largest line with about eighty pieces. All are molds from the Catalina purchase. Here again, different glazes but the same shapes. There are about ten figures in this line such as ladies and birds, but I am not fortunate enough to own any. There was a Terra Cotta line with a special stained clay body using the same figures produced from 1937-1940.

The other line made from a Catalina mold was the Nautical Art Ware. Made from 1939-1942, most of all of this series are shapes of shells. These usually have one color inside and another color outside. There were twenty-six or more and are hard to find. One is in the shape of a Dolphin.

Encanto Art Ware is an embossed group. There are two themes; one Hawaiian and the other Marine. Here again I have colors not listed in anything I researched. Twenty-five or so pieces - all vases except a rectangular box and candle holders. The Flambe is a red similar to Ruby Art but a little more orange.

Ox Blood Art Ware (saving the best for last) was in twenty-seven beautiful, different pieces produced from 1938-1942. About half of these shapes came from the Catalina molds. The color is outstanding. It was a three-fire process done with care. It is a blue inside and a little blue outside with a dark red. You must see a piece of Ox Blood and feel it to be able to enjoy its rare beauty.

Tropico Art Ware
1934-1937

Tropico was one of the first pottery organizations that Gladding, McBean & Co. purchased in Southern California. See mark section.
They made large garden urns, bird baths, hotel cigarette snuffers, flower pots and florist vases. These are difficult to find but there are a few.

These three pieces carry the Tropico mark.
6" Flower pot	$ 3.00- 7.00
5¾" Pitcher	$ 7.00- 9.00
6" Flower pot	$ 3.00- 7.00

These pieces all carry the "GMcB" mark or "Made in U.S.A.". The large leaf shaped vase is a Capistrano mold - another pottery Gladding, McBean & Company bought in Southern California. There were twelve colors and over one hundred shapes produced in this time period. Not all were from Tropico - some were original Gladding, McBean & Company molds brought from Lincoln, California.

Front Row:

Candle holder	$ 8.00-10.00
Leaf-shaped vase	$ 5.00-12.00
Bulb bowl	$ 3.00- 5.00

Top Row:

Jardiniere	$ 8.00-13.00
Vase	$ 3.00- 7.00
Utility flower vase	$ 7.00-12.00
Footed vase	$ 4.00- 6.00
Flower bowl	$ 9.00-13.00

Coronado Art Ware
1935-1942

This was made in four colors and about thirty shapes.

Footed vase, 10½″ tall, satin ivory $14.00-18.00

Low bowl, 13″, for flowers or fruit, satin ivory $15.00-20.00
Compote, satin ivory $12.00-16.00
Vase, 8½″ tall, bulbous bottom, satin ivory $14.00-18.00
9″ round bowl, satin ivory . . . . $ 8.00-12.00

These are coral and turquoise satin vases.

Front Row:

    Vase, 5 1/2" .... $ 5.00- 9.00

    Vase, 2 5/8" .... $ 6.00- 8.00

    Vase, 9 1/2" long .... $ 8.00-10.00

    Vase, 7 3/8" .... $ 7.00-12.00

Top Row:

    Vase .... $ 6.00- 8.00

    6 1/2" Candlestick .... each $ 6.00-10.00

    Footed vase .... $ 6.00- 8.00

All these pieces are in satin ivory.

    Semi-flat 13″ bowl for flowers, inside design $12.00-14.00
    Footed vase, 8″ $12.00-14.00
    Dish with lid, 5½″ $10.00-15.00
    Flat plate, 13″ . . . . $ 9.00-13.00

Candlesticks, celadon . . . . each $ 6.00- 8.00
Bowl, 14", satin ivory. (There were two bowls of
approximately the same shape and size -one
13" and one 14".) $21.00-24.00

Ruby Art Ware
1935-1936

There were twelve shapes in this line, but others were added. This is a delicate, almost china-like earthernware. The color is a bright red - really most striking. This is the After Dinner Pot and cups and saucers. These are the only pieces I have found.

After dinner pot $35.00-40.00
Cups and saucers . . . . set $15.00-18.00

Capistrano Art Ware
1936-1942

Capistrano Art Ware is a very complex line of pottery. There are six plain colors - ivory, coral, celadon, chartreuse, mauve and oatmeal. There are ten lines with double colors - one color inside and one color outside.

Front Row:

Flat vase, ivory satin underside, turquoise gloss
inside . . . . $ 4.00- 6.00

Goose on a pedestal base, oatmeal gloss $12.00-15.00

Square bowl, 4''x9¾'', celadon inside, ivory satin
underside $12.00-14.00

Square candle holders, ivory outside, celadon
inside . . . . pair $15.00-18.00

Deep bowl with grooves, ivory and turquoise $14.00-16.00

Top Row:

Leaf shaped bowl, 9¾''x14'', coral satin . . . . $ 5.00-12.00

Mauve satin rectangular bowl, 8''x11¾'' . . . . $ 9.00-15.00

Aurora and Avalon Art Ware
1937-1942

These are all from Catalina Island molds.
Shallow bowl, almost a deep plate, ivory and
   turquoise $10.00-12.00
Compote, 8" .... $ 8.00-12.00
Compote, 13" $14.00-17.00

Candle holders, satin turquoise $18.00-20.00
Flat bowl, 14¾" across $14.00-18.00

Catalina Art Ware
1937-1941

A big line of vases and a few figures, all from the Catalina Island molds. They came in many colors. There were at least seventy-eight pieces in this group. These carried an ink stamp (see mark section).

Front Row:

    Compote, ivory . . . . $ 9.00-12.00

    Small compote, two colors . . . . $ 6.00-10.00

    Graceful shell shaped vase . . . . $ 9.00-14.00

Top Row:

    Square 10" bowl, satin $12.00-14.00

    Ribbed 7¾" vase, coral satin $14.00-16.00

Encanto Art Ware
1937-1940

These had embossed designs either in a Hawaiian or a marine pattern.

Front Row:
    Bud vase, celadon . . . . $ 3.00- 5.00
    Flat vase, flambe $12.00-16.00
Top Row:
    Round vase, flambe $14.00-19.00
    Ivory cylindrical 11½" vase. (It was made in one
        other color - coral satin.) $15.00-18.00

Ox Blood Art Ware
1938-1942

This is a most unusual glaze and to me, the most beautiful. There were at least twenty-seven different shapes made in the series. About sixteen were from Catalina molds.

Lamp base with detached underplate $35.00-45.00
11" vase. (The inside is a blue - just between celadon and turquoise.) $45.00-65.00

Nautical Art Ware
1939-1942

Here we have vases all in a shell-like motif. There were twenty-six or more. Beware as there are many copies of these. This collection is made up of Catalina molds.

Front Row:
Green and gold 5½" shell vase, very special lustre
glaze. Gold on a vase is seldom found . . . . $ 9.00-15.00
Cornucopia shell vase, very graceful . . . . $ 9.00-14.00
Top Row:
Large flat shell, good quality $12.00-15.00

Specials
1934 to Present

Gladding, McBean & Co. produced thousands of pieces of Franciscan ware to be used as "give-aways". Jam jars and trays were some of the more popular "specials". The McGraw Electric of Elgin, Illinois would order up to 25,000 pieces at one time. Some organizations ordered special articles with their name on them.

New designs of Franciscan that did not fit in a certain pattern or category were listed under "specials". Perfume bottles, garden jars, battery boxes, chimney caps, insulators, culture vessels, water coolers and much more were in this group. There are about two hundred different items known.

Front Row:

Junior jam jar bottom, turquoise gloss	$ 4.00- 6.00
Condiment cup, orange gloss	$ 4.00- 6.00
Ash tray, turquoise gloss	$ 6.00- 7.00
Candle holder, ivory satin	$ 8.00-10.00
Tumbler, Mexican blue	$ 4.00- 6.00

Top Row:

Individual ramekin casserole, turquoise gloss	$ 6.00- 8.00
Jam jar, dark yellow gloss	$ 5.00- 7.00
Lid, orange gloss	$ 2.00- 3.00
Plate, dark yellow gloss	$ 3.00- 4.00
Syrup pitcher, turquoise gloss	$ 4.00- 9.00

Front Row:

    Small dish with cover, orange gloss . . . . $ 4.00- 6.00

    Hospitality tray, turquoise gloss . . . . $ 3.00- 5.00

    Sugar and creamer, solid handles, Mexican blue . $ 6.00- 8.00

Top Row:

    Deluxe jam jars (should have plate), brown gloss
      with coral gloss lid . . . . each $ 3.00- 5.00

    Butter keeper, turquoise gloss . . . . $ 9.00-12.00

    Toaster set, made for McGraw Electric, comprised
      of two jam jars - one dark yellow gloss and the
      other dark green gloss $12.00-15.00

    Plate with a place for ¼ lb. butter, dark yellow
      gloss $10.00-12.00

Front Row:
    Four different shaped trays . . . . each $ 3.00- 5.00
Top Row:
    Casserole, 8″ (should have a lid), turquoise gloss . $ 5.00- 7.00
    Ramekin, white gloss . . . . $ 3.00- 4.00
    Casserole (not supposed to have a lid), dark
       yellow gloss . . . . $ 5.00- 7.00

Front Row:
    Hospitality trays . . . . each $ 3.00- 5.00
Top Row:
    Bowl made for Sunkist $25.00-35.00

70

Hotel Wares
1937-1942

This will come as a great surprise to many of you; Gladding, Mc-Bean & Co. also made Hotel Ware. There were three different lines of Hotel Ware and all were of high quality. One of the Hotel Wares was a vitrified china and was manufactured from 1939-1942.

The first endeavor into Hotel Wares was in 1937 and continued until thirty some shapes were being produced by 1942. They came in six colors: tan, turquoise, green, dark yellow, coral, and pastel pink. These were all made in a gloss finish.

Large 10½″ sectional plate. (It was also made in a smaller size.) .... $ 9.00-12.00
Double egg cup, 3¾″ high. (It also came in a smaller size, much the same shape, and called a single egg cup.) $10.00-12.00

Front Row:

Tea cup, coral gloss glaze . . . . $ 3.00- 5.00

Saucer, turquoise gloss glaze . . . . $ 2.00- 3.00

Oval platter, 11½". (Also came in these sizes: 10
5/8", 12 5/8" and 13 5/8".) . . . . $ 7.00-11.00

After dinner saucer, but no cup . . . . $ 3.00- 4.00

7 1/8" footed salad bowl . . . . $ 5.00- 7.00

Top Row:

7 1/8" dessert plate . . . . $ 5.00- 7.00

8 1/8" salad plate . . . . $ 6.00- 7.00

Luncheon plate, 9 3/16" . . . . $ 7.00- 8.00

Butter pat between the two plates . . . . $ 7.00- 8.00

Kitchen Ware

The Kitchen Ware was comprised of around thirty pieces. There were three different shaped sets of nested mixing bowls. There were also pie plates, covered dishes and pitchers, canister sets, and icebox dishes; perhaps they were not marked and I am unable to recognize them. They were made in the bright orange and Mexican blue. As yet, I have been unable to find any of these, so this pattern is not illustrated.

Cocinero Ware
1934-1938

Some of the pieces in Cocinero Ware will have the old Tropico mark on the bottom. This might mean they were some of the molds Gladding, McBean & Co. bought in the deal when buying the Los Angeles based Tropico Co. in 1923.

There were approximately twenty pieces in the series. There are no colors listed in any literature I have been able to find. At present, I have it in Mexican blue (cobalt), turquoise, white and green; all gloss glazes. Possible more colors will be discovered.

There was a nested set of mixing bowls, perhaps six to a set. There was also a covered casserole, a batter bowl, and large salt and pepper shakers. These are hard to find.

Front Row:
    Green ramekin with lid, 2¾" deep, 5¼" across . . $ 7.00- 9.00
    Turquoise mug for punch, 2¾" tall, 3" across . . . $ 5.00- 7.00
Top Row:
    Mexican blue pitcher, 4½" tall, 3½" across . . . . . $ 6.00- 8.00
    White custard cup, 2½" high, 3 3/8" across . . . . $ 3.00- 4.00
    Turquoise pitcher, 5¾" tall, 5" across, has the
       Tropico mark on the bottom . . . . $ 7.00- 9.00

Odds and Ends

These are pieces I have that I cannot fit into a certain set or group or were left out of their proper group. Prices are not available for the items in the first two photos.

Front Row:
  The cup is an El Patio shape but color does not go with set.
  The dark green cup is in the Coronado pattern but the color is wrong.
  This saucer pattern I cannot find listed anywhere.
  Here are two more cups that are orphans.
Top Row:
  The two tumblers are unglazed on the bottom, and the color is not true - could be experimental pieces.
  The turquoise satin cup without a handle may be someone's mistake.
  The flambe platter could have been someone trying a new pattern.

Front Row:

The two pink and blue plates on each end are the original Fruit pattern, but I do not believe it was ever mass-produced in this color.

In the middle is a sculptured grape leaf or ivy plate.

Top Row:

The fat pink cup has a line drawing in a vine-like design.

The center plate is a transparent glaze with a brown and yellow edging.

The little yellow cup from the El Patio line has a small bird drawn on it.

Front Row:
    Catalina cereal, 5¼″ across, 2″ tall, satin
    turquoise inside and sand gloss outside . . . . . . $ 7.00- 9.00
    Del Oro sugar, 3¾″ across, 2¼″ tall, light blue, no
    price available.
Top Row:
    Compote, 7½″ across, 3¼″ high, turquoise gloss $ 7.00-10.00
    Coronado jam jar and lid, 3½″ high, turquoise
    gloss $12.00-15.00

Marks

TROPICO POTTERY, located on Los Feliz Boulevard, Los Angeles County, was acquired by Gladding, McBean & Co. in 1923. This stamp was used a short time after Gladding, McBean & Co. bought the plant.

These stamps are found on ware manufactured by Gladdin, Mc-Bean & Co. since 1934. Two sizes are identified with, or without, the additional "Made in USA".

The stamp MADE IN U.S.A. in two lines, is found in three sizes, very often without other identification. The largest of these stamps was also used experimently for acid imprints on dark glazes. The method was found impractical for production in 1937-38. The smallest stamp is still in use in the Earthernware Department. "Made in U.S.A." appeared in one line in 1939.

MADE IN
U.S.A

MADE IN
U. S. A.

MADE IN
U. S. A.
1

MADE IN U. S. A.

The first backstamp to indicate the Franciscan name was a square box with the capital letter "F". It was made to replace the old GMcB stamp and was used in two sizes from September 1938 to February 1939.

MADE IN
U. S. A.

MADE IN
U. S. A.

The stamp FRANCISCAN POTTERY replaced the big "F". It was later changed to read FRANCISCAN WARE which supposedly added higher prestige to the product. The stamp spelling out Franciscan Ware was used on ash trays in 1938 and on dinnerware in 1938-1939.

FRANCISCAN
+ + + WARE
MADE IN U. S. A.

FRANCISCAN
+ + POTTERY

FRANCISCAN WARE - made in California USA. ¾" and 1" stamp sizes were used from February 1939 to August 1940. A new stamp size-7/8"-was made July, 1940 and used with or without "Hand Decorated" until 1947.

These stamps are the same as the preceding except that numbers were added to the bottom for identification of the worker. They were used from 1947 to 1949.

33   17

Since there are numerous questions being asked regarding the various markings on Catalina pottery, I am going to try to enlighten you concerning a few I know.

Catalina Pottery originated on the island of Catalina, which lies in the Pacific Ocean about twenty miles from the coast of California. The island is part of Los Angeles County.

William Wrigley, Jr. bought the island in 1920 and developed part of it as a resort. In 1930 there was a need to employ the local Indians and others and since there were clay deposits on the island the pottery idea was developed.

The name Catalina or Catalina Island was inscribed on the back of the pottery by hand with a sharp pointed tool. Other impressions were made in case molds at a later date. There were four or so of these, the most prevalent being in a horizontal direction. Impressions were made with a pointed tool.

Catalina
Island

Catalina

CATALINA

CATALINA
ISLAND
624

CATALINA

CATALINA
60
ND

In April of 1937, Gladding, McBean & Co. purchased Catalina Pottery. This purchase included the ware in stock, 174 molds and the right to continue the name. After 1937, the identification on the back appeared printed in ink.

The Gladding, McBean & Co. produced a dinner ware line along with the other Catalina pieces and added many other shapes. There were three main stamps used between 1937 and 1942. One stamp incorporated the word RANCHO with the Catalina.

There is very little similarity in the Island-produced and the Mainland-produced pieces. The quality of the clay is entirely different. The clay quality was the main reason for selling the Island Pottery.

These marks were used on the bottom of each piece after the move to the Mainland:

CATALINA
C 806
POTTERY

CATALINA
RANCHO

Impressions made starting in 1937.

CATALINA
MADE IN
U. S. A.
POTTERY

CATALINA
MADE IN
U. S. A.
POTTERY

CATALINA
MADE IN
U.S.A.
POTTERY

CATALINA
REG. U. S.
PAT. OFF.
RANCHO

CATALINA
REG. U. S.
PAT. OFF.
RANCHO

Backstamps printed with ink, 1937 to 1942.